FEARFULLY AND WONDERFULLY MADE:

Remembering South Africa, I Didn't Know That I was Beautiful (But I Know Now), White Gaze, I Grew Up on Rosa Parks and more

REV. LADONNA SANDERS NKOSI

Contact Publications at connect@thegatheringchicago.org

ISBN: 978-1-7367371-0-1

Published by Rev. LaDonna Sanders Nkosi, Chicago, USA

Cover Photo Credit: Rev. LaDonna Sanders Nkosi "Sunrise Over the Indian Ocean" at South Beach, Durban, South Africa.

Author Photo on back cover: Imagery by Chioma, www.imagerybychioma.com

Cover layout and internal layout by Divine Flow Publishing, Ltd.

"For you created my inmost being. You knit me together in my mother's womb. I praise you because I am fearfully and wonderfully made. Wonderful are your works God. I know that full well." Psalm 139:13-14

To the one who;
thought you were not beautiful,
thought you were not enough,
thought you were too much…
This is for you.

Your life matters.
Our lives matter.
You matter.
And you are beautiful.
You are fearfully and wonderfully made.
#Psalm139

Contents

Acknowledgments

To all my kin, by blood and otherwise. To the Phillips Sisters and Brothers of Washington, Arkansas (and their descendants) who migrated in pairs and threes to Kansas City and beyond. To Ms. Mary Ellen Laden, my high school English teacher who encouraged my poetic voice and writing gifts when not everyone else did. To Dr. Joanne M. Terrell. To the teachers, community, and the village, and all those who see and nurture greatness in children and people through every stage.

To the one who birthed me, literally and otherwise, Mama Alma Marie Martin. Thank you for giving me life and for nurturing me into who I have become. Thank you for editing this volume of poetry, and for always being here to cheer me on. Upon reading "Tribute to Mrs. Rosa Parks" for the first time, you said, "Did you write this?" I said, "Yes, Mom." And you said, "Wow, you are really Young, Gifted and Black." Thank you for all your love and affirmation at just the right time.

To Faith in Action, Durban, South Africa, The Gathering Chicago and The Gathering Global Network, thank you for your faithfulness, love, community and living expressions of *UBUNTU*.

To Camelle Daley, founder of House of ilona Clergy brand and author of *Finding Divine Flow.* And to artist and community leader Jeffery Beckham, Jr. of artbyjeffbeckham.com Thank you both for calling forth the artist in me at just the right time. You inspired me to create more and publish through your bold, unapologetic and faithful creation and distribution of your artwork.

I count myself blessed to be alive, awake, equipped and called for these times. When I was younger, I dreamed of one day being called, "Poet." With publishing of this collection you are reading, I can say, that's what I am.

Acknowledgments

To all my kin, by blood and otherwise. To the Phillips Sisters and Brothers of Washington, Arkansas (and their descendants) who migrated in pairs and threes to Kansas City and beyond. To Ms. Mary Ellen Laden, my high school English teacher who encouraged my poetic voice and writing gifts when not everyone else did. To Dr. Joanne M. Terrell. To the teachers, community, and the village, and all those who see and nurture greatness in children and people through every stage.

To the one who birthed me, literally and otherwise, Mama Alma Marie Martin. Thank you for giving me life and for nurturing me into who I have become. Thank you for editing this volume of poetry, and for always being here to cheer me on. Upon reading "Tribute to Mrs. Rosa Parks" for the first time, you said, "Did you write this?" I said, "Yes, Mom." And you said, "Wow, you are really Young, Gifted and Black." Thank you for all your love and affirmation at just the right time.

To Faith in Action, Durban, South Africa, The Gathering Chicago and The Gathering Global Network, thank you for your faithfulness, love, community and living expressions of *UBUNTU*.

To Camelle Daley, founder of House of ilona Clergy brand and author of *Finding Divine Flow.* And to artist and community leader Jeffery Beckham, Jr. of artbyjeffbeckham.com Thank you both for calling forth the artist in me at just the right time. You inspired me to create more and publish through your bold, unapologetic and faithful creation and distribution of your artwork.

I count myself blessed to be alive, awake, equipped and called for these times. When I was younger, I dreamed of one day being called, "Poet." With publishing of this collection you are reading, I can say, that's what I am.

1

Remembering South Africa

Singing: Sivusilele Nkosi Jesu
Revive us, again O God.
Revive us again.

Suddenly
In remembering South Africa,
I'm in love with my skin again.

Suddenly,
In remembering South Africa.
I'm in love with my skin again.

Brown, Black, Rich, Sweet,

Brilliant, Me.

Suddenly, in remembering South Africa
I'm in love with my skin again.
And I miss that
Here.

I miss that here
Where Black is black,
A spot in a sea of whiteness.
An accident,
A mishap,
An oversight,

And we must hide her.
And she hides herself
Behind stacks and stacks of books
And many big words
And many degrees
And high-powered positions.

But suddenly,
In remembering South Africa
I'm in love with my skin again,
Where the curve-ness
And the round-ness
And brown-ness
Of me is beautiful
is expected
is beloved
is beheld
baked, brown, round,
and Beautiful Me.

Suddenly,
In remembering South Africa,
I'm in love with my skin again.
And somehow the South African water
Didn't dry or ash my skin over
But the climate conditioned me
And I was vibrant and supple and alive.

And my hair just grew and grew and grew and grew
From the nurture and nourishment there.

And coal brown eyes
That pierce with expression,
They were not the exception
but the rule.

And more than every other person
Looked just like me.

O suddenly in Remembering South Africa
I'm in love with my skin again.
And I am alive again
And I am renewed again
And I am radiant again
And I am beautiful again
And I am born again
And I am me again

Amen

2

I Didn't Know That I Was Beautiful (But I Know Now)

I didn't know that I was beautiful
I felt small, and insignificant,
In the grand scheme of things.

I was born into a world where black
had to get back, brown could stick around
but white was right.
I didn't know that I was beautiful.

Even among my own people
There have been skin gradations
We've made our own classifications and separations
and being dark brown and round

I didn't know I was beautiful.

I didn't know that I was beautiful.

That my skin was more than ash and ugly and unmatterable

I felt that I had to make up for my shortcomings

My relegation to second- and third-class citizen ship

My ancestors came in on ships as

Precious cargo

I didn't know I was beautiful.

I didn't know that I was beautiful.

That I had Harriet Tubman in my veins

and the locks of Sojourner Truth in my hair

I didn't know that my daddy had the hands of Denmark Vesey

And that the preach of Gabriel Prosser had been ringin' in my ears.

I didn't know the blood of Malcolm has been pulsing

In my indignation and in the power of my vocals as I protest the insanity.

I didn't know I was beautiful.

And I didn't even know Nelson Mandela
or Queen Nzinga
or Nana Yaa Asantewaa

I didn't know I was beautiful
I didn't know who I was
I didn't know where I came from.

He doesn't know that he is beautiful.
That he is powerful.
That his life means something.
That the Spirit of God pulses through his veins.
That his hands and heart are blessed.
That he was made on purpose.
He is made on purpose.
We were made on purpose.
You are made on purpose.

You are beautiful
beautiful
beautiful.
Beautiful
black

caramel

cream

milk

mocha brown

milk

chocolate

coffee

cocoa Black

cappuccino

frappuccino

You

are

beautiful.

um hum

With every angle

And every curve

And every line

And your roundness

And Brown-ness

And Strength

and Your complexities

Every detail

Fearfully and Wonderfully Made:

You, my Beloved are made in the image
of Almighty God.
You are beautiful.
You are beautiful.

You are fearfully and wonderfully made.
Somebody say, I am fearfully and wonderfully made.
I am fearfully and wonderfully made.
I am beautiful.
I didn't know that I was beautiful,
but I know now.

3

Tribute to Mrs. Rosa Parks

I grew up on Rosa Parks

I grew up on Rosa Parks

I grew up on Grandma's chicken

And collard greens and

I grew up on Rosa Parks

I grew up on Rosa Parks and was a benefactor of her reality

The first woman of Montgomery's NAACP

A seamstress, they said was quiet

But with one move to step out of racist expectation

She shook up the nation

The whole of creation

I Grew Up on Rosa Parks

And I grew up on the fact that the purposeful action
Of ordinary everyday people could change the courses
Of nations, the whole of Civilization
Could shake the bedrock of the confederation
I Grew Up on Rosa Parks

And I Grew up on Run DMC
And Public Enemy
And I grew up On Rosa Parks

And she taught us that
You don't have to say much to shake up nations
To shake the foundations of
Jim Crow Segregation
That sometimes it's not what you say about freedom
But what you do about freedom
Not what you say about change
But what you do about change
Can't always stay safe about change
Got to do somethin' about change
Got to say somethin' about change

You know we reap the benefits of privilege

And then want to say somebody ought to do somethin' 'bout the way we're livin'

What they gone do about the way we're livin'.

But we grew up on Rosa Parks

We grew up on Rosa Parks

And The Revolution is not a Spectator Sport

The Revolution is not a Spectator Sport

We Grew up on Rosa Parks

But who will the babies and the brothers and the sisters grow up on?

Who will the babies and the brothers and sisters grow up on?

Who will they say stood up, sat down, spoke up, organized, institutionalized

Me? You?

We Grew up on Rosa Parks…Who by her actions said, "Let My People go!"

"Let My People go!"

From Moses to Jesus to Malcolm and Betty to Rosa to Martin and Coretta to Mandela.

From Moses to Jesus to Malcolm and Betty to Rosa to Martin and Coretta to Mandela.

They said "Let my people Go."

"Let my people Go."

But I say,

When they let us go, what will we do?

When they let us go,

What will we do?

Let us let our our lives and actions be monuments to Mrs. Rosa Parks

To the Forerunners

And the ancestors.

This is a Tribute to Mrs. Rosa Parks.

4

The White Gaze

(May 2020, somewhere after
the murder of Mr. George Floyd)
Preamble: We Are a Great People

I see you. I see you Staring down at me
Knee on my neck
Menacing scowl of one who is to
Serve and Protect
I see you.

I see you. I am somewhere in the White Gaze
The social media Gaze
Where people are dissecting and criticizing

And hiding and blaming
And passing the buck

Oh, I see you.
I am somewhere in the White Gaze
The political and media Haze
An afternoon run
father and son
Run me down, shoot me down
And remain free
I see you

I see you
I am blinded by the White Gaze
The lamenting Haze
The guilt phase
You feel sorry for me blaze
But continue to say and do nothing.
Gunned down in my own house.
I see you.

Oh, I see you
I see you

Staring down on me

Black body charred by you

Tied to a railroad track

Smoldering flesh

And you in your Sunday best

I see you.

I see you.

We see you.

God sees you.

This is the White Gaze.

5

Remembering Who We Are

Singing and Praying:
Be still and know that I am God.
Be still and know that I am God.
Be still and know. Be still. Be.
I am the Lord that healeth thee.
I am the Lord that healeth thee.

Born a beloved child of God

Before I even knew so

Before I was even thought of

Before the foundations of the world

I, a baby girl, just above the toddling age

Sank my bare tippy toes in deep plush red carpets,

I stepped my feet on deep plush

Red carpets and step by step passed ornate thrones and seats of gold and crimson.

I dragged the plushness of my yellow and gold calico baby blanket down the aisle

Stepping on deep red carpets and the harps played and trumpets sounded

As I stepped up one, two, three

To the Throne of Grace

And all glory shone from the seat of the throne

And I climbed up on the lap of the

Creator

And God whispered in my ear…

God said,

Before you are born,

Know that I know you

Before I put you in the womb

Know that I have set you apart

I appoint you as a prophet to the nations

God said,

Fear not for I have redeemed you

I have called you by name

You are mine.

When you pass through the waters

I will be with you

When you walk through fire you will not be burned.

At times you will forget,

But it is me who knit you together in your mother's womb,

At times you will forget,

But you are fear-fully and wonderfully made.

Wonderful are my works.

Know that full well.

Born a beloved child of God

Before you even knew so

Before you were even thought of

Before the foundations of the world

You, a baby boy, a baby girl, just above the toddling age

Sank your bare tippy toes in deep plush red carpets,

You stepped your feet on deep plush

Red carpets and step by step passed ornate thrones and seats of gold and crimson.

You dragged the plushness, your favorite baby blanket down the aisle.

Stepping on deep red carpets and the harps played and trumpets sounded

As you stepped up one, two, three
To the Throne of Grace
And all glory shone from the seat of the throne
As you climbed up on the lap of the Creator
And God whispered in your ear…

Remember?
Remember?
Remember?

Remember.

This is Remembering Who We Are.

About the Author

Rev. LaDonna Sanders Nkosi is the founder of The Gathering Chicago and the Gathering Global Network based in Hyde Park, Chicago with members and partners from around the world; from South Africa to Rwanda to Swaziland to the United States to the United Kingdom.

Born in Kansas City, Missouri, Rev. LaDonna began writing in the fourth grade at age nine and discovered her poetic voice in high school. At university and early in her career, she lost touch with poetry as a journalist and technical writer. But when she first set foot on the land and shores of Durban, South Africa, the rivers of poetry began to flow once again.

In 2003, Rev. LaDonna was the first US American woman ordained for international ministry in Durban, South Africa. A committed global bridge-builder and catalyst, she has sojourned to South Africa 12 times on partnership and bridgebuilding journeys.

These days, Rev. LaDonna is hosting the Healing Racism Journaling Experience and is completing her Doctorate as Wright Scholar in African-Centered Ministries and Theology at McCormick Theological Seminary where she also holds a Master of Divinity. She received a Master of Arts in Interdisciplinary Studies in African American Studies and Women's Studies from DePaul University and a Bachelor of Journalism in Advertising and Public Relations from the University of Missouri School of Journalism.

Rev. LaDonna is a Founders Coach, Mentor and Dream Midwife for leaders, creatives and change agents from around the world. She hosts virtual retreats and empowerment gatherings globally and locally. For coaching, keynote speaking, and for bookings contact connect@thegatheringchicago.org.

Fearfully and Wonderfully Made is a poetic prophetic declaration. In spite of pervasive racism and challenges, we are made in the image of God, formed and fashioned exactly for transforming these times.

Much of Rev. LaDonna's poetry has been inspired by her journeys from the U.S. to South Africa and back again. These include "Remembering South Africa" and "I didn't Know I was Beautiful (But I Know Now)." "The White Gaze" came just days after the public video murder of Mr. George Floyd.

Rev. LaDonna writes:

"May we all be strengthened, restored and empowered on the inside and the outside, as we arise to be a part of transformation in these times. We've been made for such a time as this. Thank you for reading. God blessings multiplied!"

Rev. LaDonna Sanders Nkosi,

Hyde Park, Chicago, Feb. 2021.

www.thegatheringchicago.org

www.ingramcontent.com/pod-product-compliance
Lightning Source LLC
LaVergne TN
LVHW050950080826
845145LV00004B/1459

* 9 7 8 1 7 3 6 7 3 7 1 0 1 *